JOSEPH HAYDN

CANZONETTAS AND SONGS
KANZONETTEN UND LIEDER

for Voice and Piano / für Gesang und Klavier

Edited by / Herausgegeben von
Ludwig Landshoff

EIGENTUM DES VERLEGERS · ALLE RECHTE VORBEHALTEN
ALL RIGHTS RESERVED

C.F. PETERS CORPORATION
LONDON · LEIPZIG · NEW YORK

PREFACE

Connoisseurs relegate Haydn's Songs to a position of somewhat secondary importance and music-enthusiasts, generally speaking, know little or nothing of the master's very considerable attainments in this branch of his art.

Incidental and adverse circumstances have been largely responsible for the obscurity of these songs, these valuable and important treasures of musical art have, for this reason, lain fallow practically up to the present day.

At the time of their first publication contemporary musicians were prone to adopt towards them an attitude of rigid asceticism, following this up with a lack of appreciation for their intrinsic value. In the prevailing contention between poet and composer, between words and music, popular opinion had once again turned in favour of the poet.

Johann Abraham Peter Schulz, a fervent protagonist of the new art-song in Germany, expressed the following opinion:—

"The ultimate aim and object of a writer of songs is to popularize good texts,—a melodic line in itself is not sufficient—it should, moreover, enhance the meaning of the words and thus attract interest to the vocal line, in this way the memory and the musical feelings of the listener will be more deeply affected. Superflous embellishments and fussiness in the treatment of the melodic line and its accompaniment, unnecessary padding and reiterated statements (whereby the main interest is sacrificed to secondary details, for instance, words to music or vice-versa), such details cannot be deprecated strongly enough and they are entirely unnecessary."

It is interesting to note that Haydn tackled the whole question from a different point of view.

He had had, either as a chorister of St Stephen's church or later as conductor to the Court at Esterhaz, practically no opportunity of a literary education, he seemed strongly inclined on one hand to write songs of an arch or affectionate type, on the other those of a gay or sorrowful nature and for such purposes he had resorted to poems in great variety which had been selected for him by his publisher and personal friends in Vienna.

Apart from this he evinced no special interest in the personality of the writer or of his work,— he did not even consider it necessary to quote the author's name in his collection of songs and contrary to the practice of his musical colleagues in the north of Germany he felt, moreover, justified in making greater demands on the poetic content of the words in order to satisfy his own idea of musical form and its many requirements.

He complains, moreover, — "that our German poets do not write sufficiently *musical* language, they are not particular enough in their choice of vowel sounds, — their verses lack uniformity of mood, their gist being conclusive in one line and inconclusive in the other corresponding to it".

To a man of humble parentage and simple environment, who right up to his later years was imbued with the feeling of folksong inculcated during his youth amidst homely surroundings, a song simply conveyed a lyric composed of verses.

It is, therefore, simple to understand why he generally adheres to the verse-structure in his settings, in the more general layout of his work he is, however more concerned with the musical material and its development.

It was not before he had reached his fiftieth year that he started to concentrate his entire energies on the composition of songs and it is not surprising that such a strong and resolute personality should be unable to thwart its creative instincts and subordinate its art to the demands of the poet.

Trained as he was in the art of Bel Canto by Porpora, well versed in the most diverse forms of orchestration and by now a mature artist, the time had come when he felt he must give rein to inspirations engendered by verse and imbue this new experience with all his prowess and artistry.

His method of song-writing was, therefore, bound to provoke adverse criticism from his somewhat narrow-minded literary contemporaries.

They argued that with such superficial management of the voice part, a clear reproduction of the words of the poem was bound to suffer, that, moreover, he swamped the words by too heavy an acompaniment.

J. F. Reichardt, a composer and very able critic of the time, summed up public opinion in a review of Haydn's third volume of songs as follows:—

"However obvious an appeal these songs may make to listeners accustomed to florid and bizarre effects, however well they may be interpreted by a consummate voice or skilfully played by an expert accompanist, it is not possible to class these compositions as "Lieder". A song should be simple in form and line,—it should permit the unfettered use of a competent voice and allow the instrumental accompaniment, however indispensable, to act as a background in complete subordination to the vocal line."

The passage of time, bringing with it the development of the Art song during the 19th century, tended to modify Reichardt's somewhat sweeping verdict.

Haydn undoubtedly deserves the credit of having elevated the "Lied" from a mass of prejudice and pedantry to a standard of higher development, he liberated it from the zeal of the poet and restored to the composer the right to imbue it with the outcome of his own imagination.

This fact would certainly have been recognized after Schubert's death and Haydn's songs, with special reference to the later examples, would have received greater recognition had not the last two sets been published in such a terribly distorted form. He had set these songs to English words during his last two sojourns in London and had had them published in two sets of "Six original Canzonettas".

Of this fact and of the existence of the original London engravings (with the original texts) Germany was kept in ignorance. The consequence was that musical Germany became acquainted with pitiable translations and was unable to fathom how an artist of Haydn's stature "could stoop to setting such inferior poetry to music" (Reichardt).

And what seemed worse, their so-called musical treatment was bound to offend, not to mention their meaningless texts, which neither in contents, structure or rhyming qualities seemed to conform to their English prototypes.

Single movements would appear incoherently separated by interludes, accents, phrasing marks, rests, even the termination of the song seemed to have no definite connection with the music, turns of melody characteristic of the composer would occur under words of quite secondary importance, sforzando- and marks of expression were quite out of place and added to all this were sudden and unexpected transitions to unrelated keys and a host of other discrepancies too numerous to mention.

It is true that the Artaria Edition printed the English text below the vocal line in the six canzonettas of the second set, this was considered of secondary importance.

The title used misleads in itself,—"Six Songs... with German and English Text", This would undoubtedly produce the impression that the German version was original and the English version a translation of it.

The first complete edition compiled by Breitkopf and Haertel during Haydn's lifetime,—the two volumes of songs, Books 8 and 9, had been published in 1803—produced the first six English Canzonettas in the same version as that of the Artaria Edition, the subsequent ones had been revised and translated somewhat better, yet they omitted to reproduce the original English text.

This version again served as a model for subsequent editions as well as a basis for Peters' Edition, which at the time was the only one in circulation and use. Thus had the German public been duped into believing that Haydn was responsible for setting these wretched, piecemeal verses to music, a version which entirely ignored every consideration of language and which was entirely lacking in every nuance of declamation, rhythm, sound or accent.

The editor's primary interest, therefore, was to submit an entirely new edition of the 12 Canzonettas and of two further English songs, Nos. 13 and 14, to supply these with the original text and further to furnish them with suitably "vocal" translations, which should adhere to the original text as closely as possible and carefully follow the vocal line.

It is some time ago that I published the first six English Canzonettas in their original form and added to them a new German translation by Karl Wolfskehl, apart from supplying the preface with detailed information regarding Haydn's song activities, it was a first attempt at classification and, as such, an effort to bring order out of confusion*).

By kind permission of the author and of the Drei Masken Verlag these translations have here been reprinted as Nos. 1—6.

The English version of the Canzonettas, Nos. 7 to 12, as well as the two English songs, "The Spirit's Song", No. 13, and "O tuneful voice", No. 14, the revision of the German text belonging to the Italian song "Un tetto umil", have all been carried out by Franz Hessel who with my collaboration adapted them to Haydn's music.

The two songs — "In nomine Domini" and "Song of Farewell", belonging to the 35 numbers of this edition, are here published for the first time. For reference, see remarks relating to Nos. 33 and 34 at the end of the volume.

The songs of the first two sets are with two exceptions designated "Pianoforte Songs" — equally suitable as songs or pieces for solo-pianoforte, the original Artaria and the old complete Breitkopf and Haertel Editions had these engraved on two separate stave-systems.

I felt consequently that I was not justified in modifying this mode of notation, as it seemed questionable whether the pianist when accompanying is supposed to play all the notes printed in the top stave of the uppermost system.

Most of the melodic embellishments are obviously only intended for the pianist, the present edition, however, gives in parentheses such ornaments *not* intended for the singer.

The small appoggiatura notes, for the notation of which Haydn as well as the original versions seemed to have shown but scanty consideration, have been written out in full. They are based on the actual execution of the period.

My own additions regarding marks of expression and articulation are easily recognized by the employment of finer print.

I should like to conclude by tendering my sincere thanks to the following governing bodies for their unfailing courtesy and kindness in placing at my disposal original autographs, copies and engravings: —
The Music Departments of: —
The Prussian State Library and Castle Library in Berlin,
the Bavarian State Library in Munich,
the National Library in Vienna
and also to express my deep appreciation of services rendered by Dr. Hugo Botstiber and Anton v. Hoboken, both resident in Vienna.

Ludwig Landshoff

---

*) Joseph Haydn, English Canzonettas with an introduction and edited by Ludwig Landshoff, 1924. "Musikalische Stundenbücher" of the Drei Masken Verlag.

INHALT / CONTENTS

Kanzonetten und Lieder / Canzonettas and Songs

No.			Page
1.	The Mermaid's Song	Die Seejungfer	1
2.	Recollection	Rückerinnerung	5
3.	A Pastoral Song	Schäferlied	9
4.	Despair	Verzweiflung	13
5.	Pleasing Pains	Verliebte Pein	16
6.	Fidelity	Treue	19
7.	Sailors' Song	Englisches Matrosenlied	24
8.	The Wanderer	Der Wanderer	27
9.	Sympathy	Sympathie	30
10.	She never told her love	Die Liebe trug sie stumm	33
11.	Piercing Eyes	Heller Blick	35
12.	Content	Genügsamkeit	37
13.	The Spirit's Song	Des Geistes Gesang	41
14.	O tuneful Voice	O Stimme hold	44

⟨deutsche Übersetzung von K. Wolfskehl und F. Hessel⟩

Deutsche Lieder / German Songs

No.		Page
15.	Eine sehr gewöhnliche Geschichte	49
16.	Die Verlassene	50
17.	Der Gleichsinn	51
18.	An Thyrsis	52
19.	Trost unglücklicher Liebe	53
20.	Die Landlust	55
21.	Die zu späte Ankunft der Mutter	56
22.	Jeder meint, der Gegenstand	57
23.	Lachet nicht, Mädchen	58
24.	Gegenliebe	59
25.	Gebet zu Gott	60
26.	Auch die Sprödeste der Schönen	62
27.	Zufriedenheit	63
28.	Das Leben ist ein Traum	64
29.	Lob der Faulheit	66
30.	Auf meines Vaters Grab	67
31.	Un tetto umil — Ein kleines Haus	68
32.	Antwort auf die Frage eines Mädchens — Pensi a me sì fido amante	71
33.	In nomine Domini — Trachten will ich nicht auf Erden	74
34.	Abschiedslied	75
35.	Gott, erhalte den Kaiser	77

The Mermaids Song / Die Seejungfer

Joseph Haydn (1732-1809)
Anne Hunter

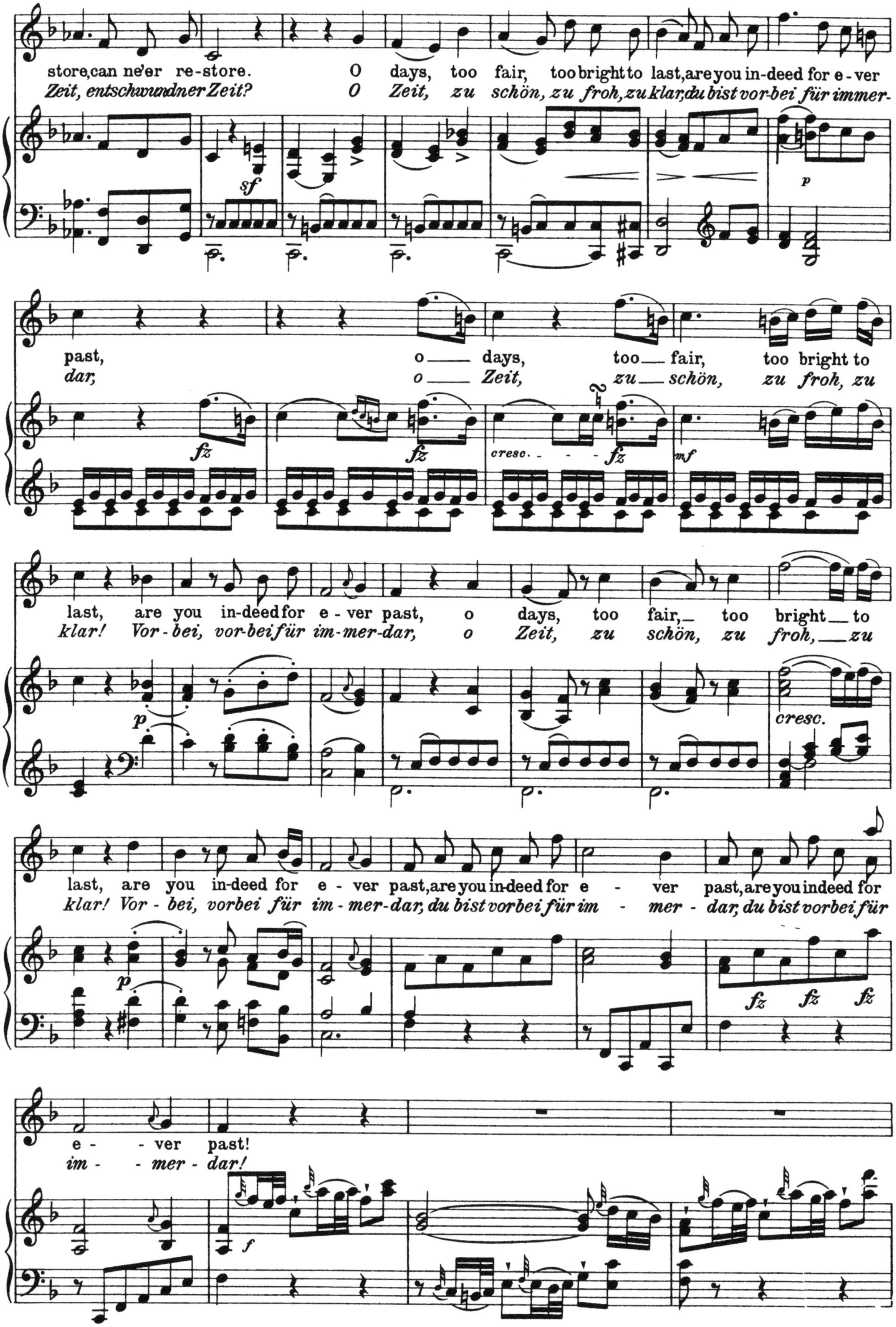
store, can ne'er re-store. O days, too fair, too bright to last, are you in-deed for e-ver
Zeit, entschwundner Zeit? O Zeit, zu schön, zu froh, zu klar, du bist vor-bei für immer-
sf
p
past, o days, too fair, too bright to
dar, o Zeit, zu schön, zu froh, zu
fz fz cresc. fz mf
last, are you in-deed for e-ver past, o days, too fair, too bright to
klar! Vor-bei, vor-bei für im-mer-dar, o Zeit, zu schön, zu froh, zu
p cresc.
last, are you in-deed for e-ver past, are you in-deed for e-ver past, are you indeed for
klar! Vor-bei, vorbei für im-mer-dar, du bist vorbei für im-mer-dar, du bist vorbei für
p fz fz fz
e-ver past!
im-mer-dar!
f

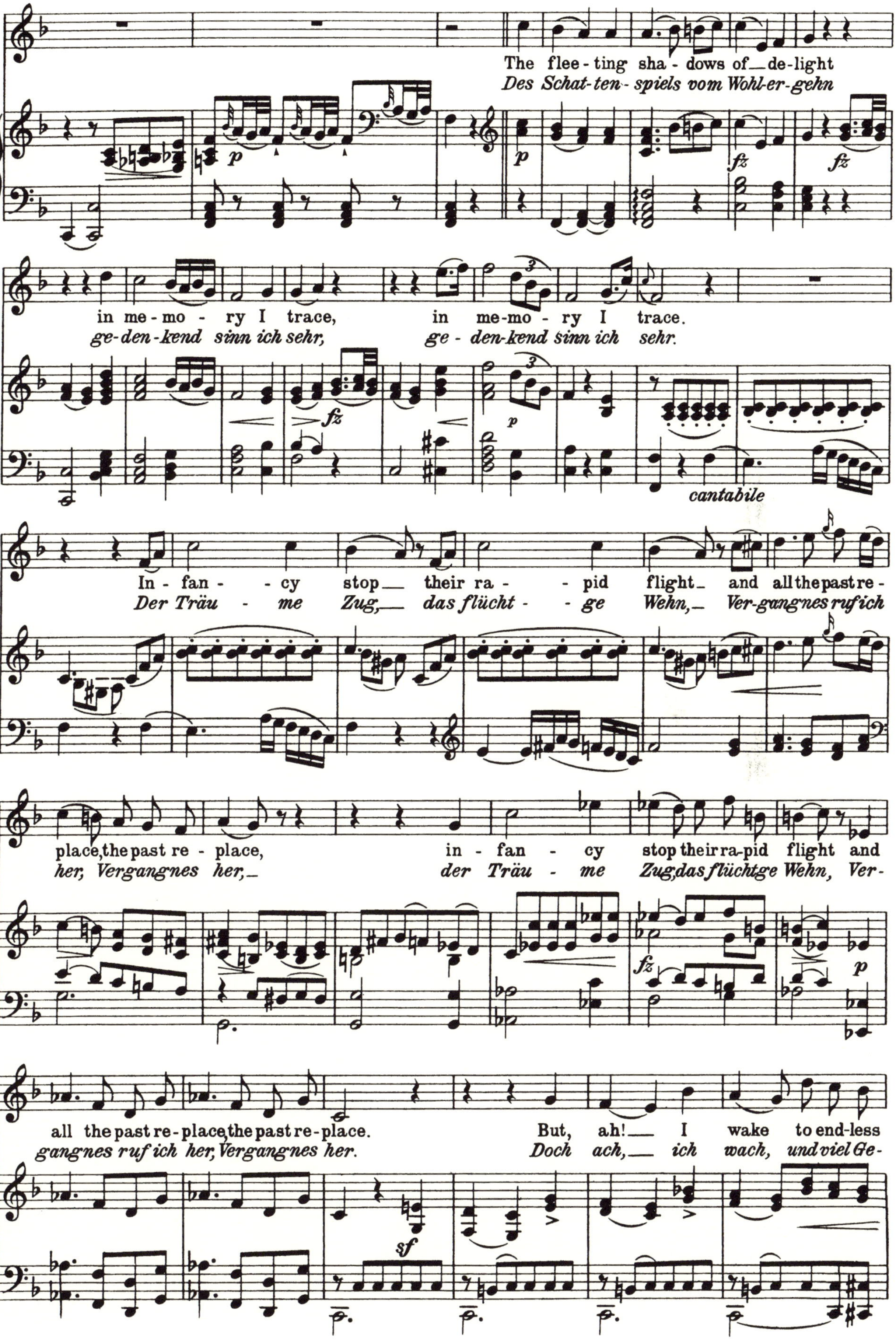
The flee-ting sha-dows of — de-light
Des Schat-ten-spiels vom Wohl-er-gehn
in me-mo-ry I trace, in me-mo-ry I trace.
ge-den-kend sinn ich sehr, ge-den-kend sinn ich sehr.
cantabile
In-fan-cy stop — their ra-pid flight — and all the past re-
Der Träu-me Zug, — das flücht-ge Wehn, — Ver-gangnes ruf ich
place, the past re-place, in-fan-cy stop their ra-pid flight and
her, Vergangnes her, — der Träu-me Zug das flüchtge Wehn, Ver-
all the past re-place, the past re-place. But, ah! — I wake to end-less
gangnes ruf ich her, Vergangnes her. Doch ach, — ich wach, und viel Ge-

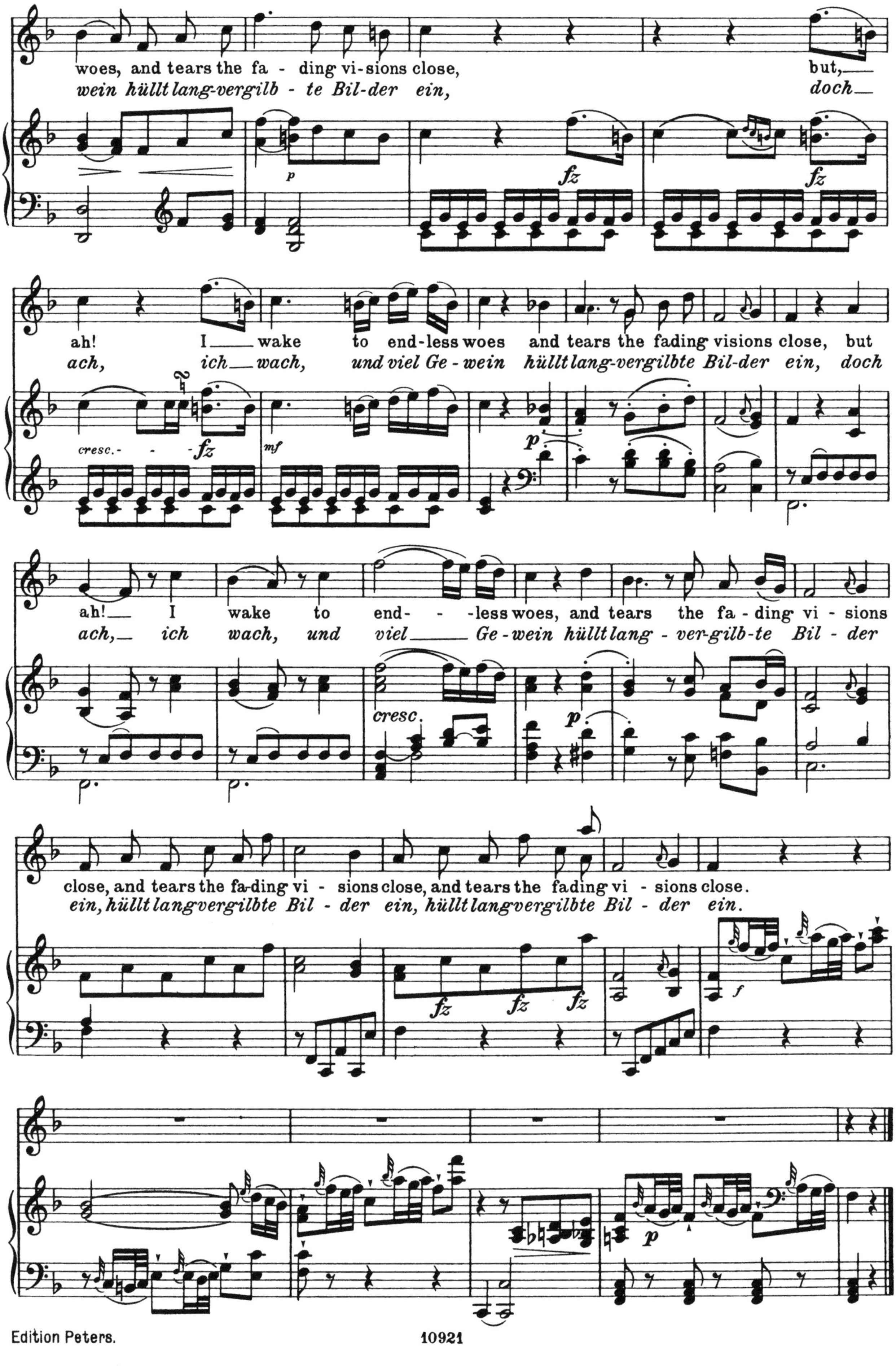
woes, and tears the fa - ding vi-sions close, but,
wein hüllt lang-vergilb - te Bil-der ein, doch
p
fz
fz
ah! I wake to end-less woes and tears the fading visions close, but
ach, ich wach, und viel Ge-wein hüllt lang-vergilbte Bil-der ein, doch
cresc. - - fz
mf
p
ah! I wake to end- - less woes, and tears the fa - ding vi - sions
ach, ich wach, und viel Ge-wein hüllt lang - ver-gilb-te Bil - der
cresc.
p
close, and tears the fa-ding vi - sions close, and tears the fading vi - sions close.
ein, hüllt langvergilbte Bil - der ein, hüllt langvergilbte Bil - der ein.
fz fz fz
f
p

A Pastoral Song / Schäferlied

Anne Hunter

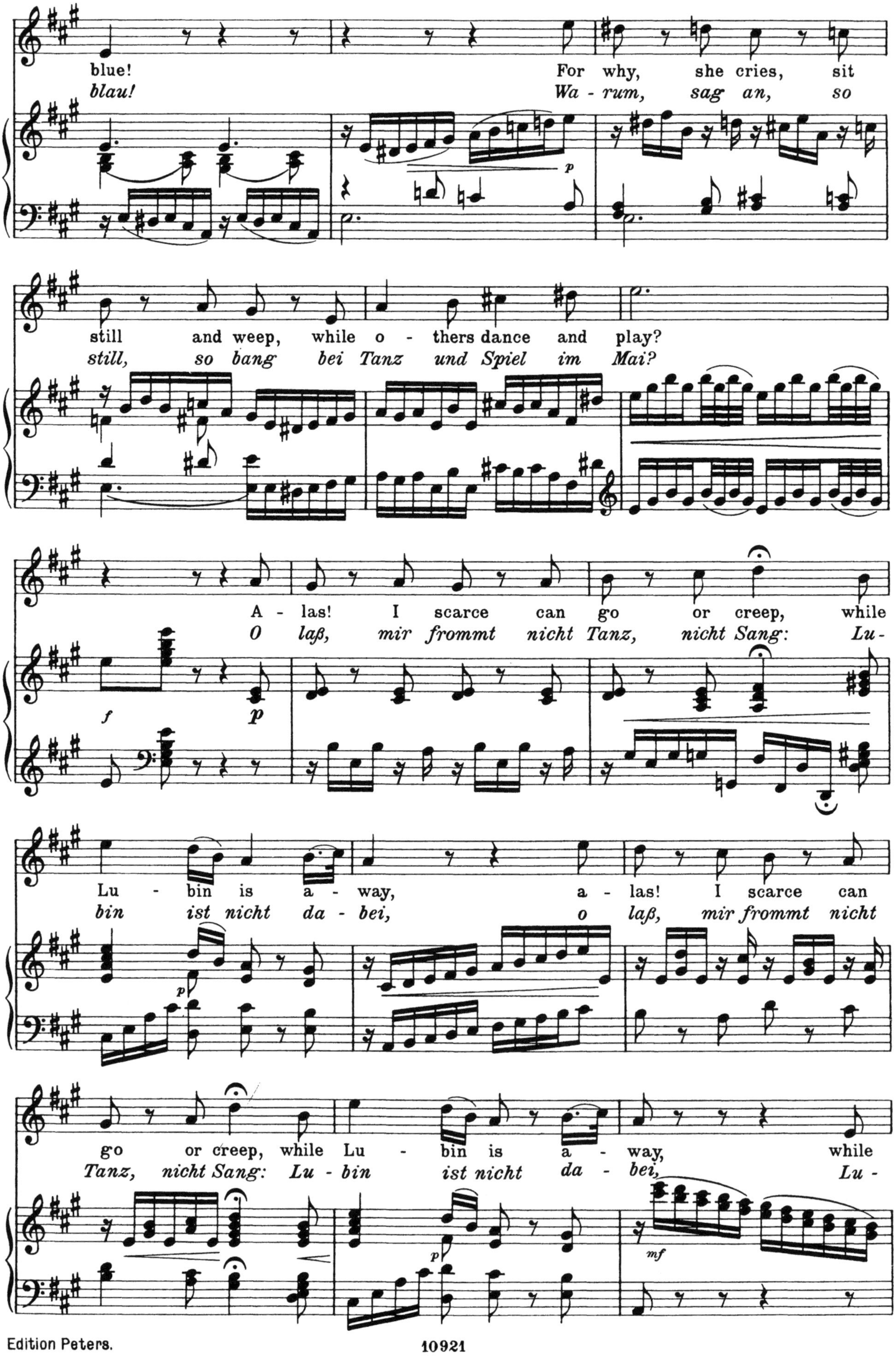
blue! For why, she cries, sit
blau! Wa - rum, sag an, so
still and weep, while o - thers dance and play?
still, so bang bei Tanz und Spiel im Mai?
f
p
A - las! I scarce can go or creep, while
O laß, mir frommt nicht Tanz, nicht Sang: Lu -
Lu - bin is a - way, a - las! I scarce can
bin ist nicht da - bei, o laß, mir frommt nicht
go or creep, while Lu - bin is a - way, while
Tanz, nicht Sang: Lu - bin ist nicht da - bei, Lu -
mf

11

Lu - bin is a - way, is a - way, is a - way.
bin ist nicht da - bei, nicht da - bei, nicht da - bei.

'Tis sad to think the days are gone, when those we love were near, I
Voll Trauer denk ich manchen Tag, der mir in Lieb ge-lacht. Auf

sit up - on this mos - sy stone and sigh when none can hear,
morschem Stein ich sitz und klag al - lein oft Tag und Nacht,

I sit up - on this mos - sy stone and sigh, and sigh when none can
auf morschem Stein ich sitz und klag al - lein, al - lein oft Tag und

hear. And while I spin my
Nacht. Und spinn ich dann den

Despair / Verzweiflung

Anne Hunter

3. Yet, if at eve, you chance to stray,
   Where silent sleeps the peacefull dead,
   Give to your kind compassion way,
   Nor check the tears by pity shed.

4. When e'er the precious dew drop falls
   I ne'er can know, I ne'er can see;
   And if sad thought my fate recalls,
   A sigh may rise unheard by me.

*Doch wenn du nachts hinwanderst einst,
Wo Tröster Tod mein Leid gestillt,
Die Träne, die um mich du weinst,
Laß rinnen sie, die fühlend quillt.*

*Wenn einst solch heilger Tau sich senkt,
Spürt nichts mein Sinn, mein blind Gesicht;
Wenn Schwermut trüb einst mein gedenkt,
Wenn Seufzen klagt, ich hör es nicht.*

Edition Peters.

Fidelity / Treue

Anne Hunter

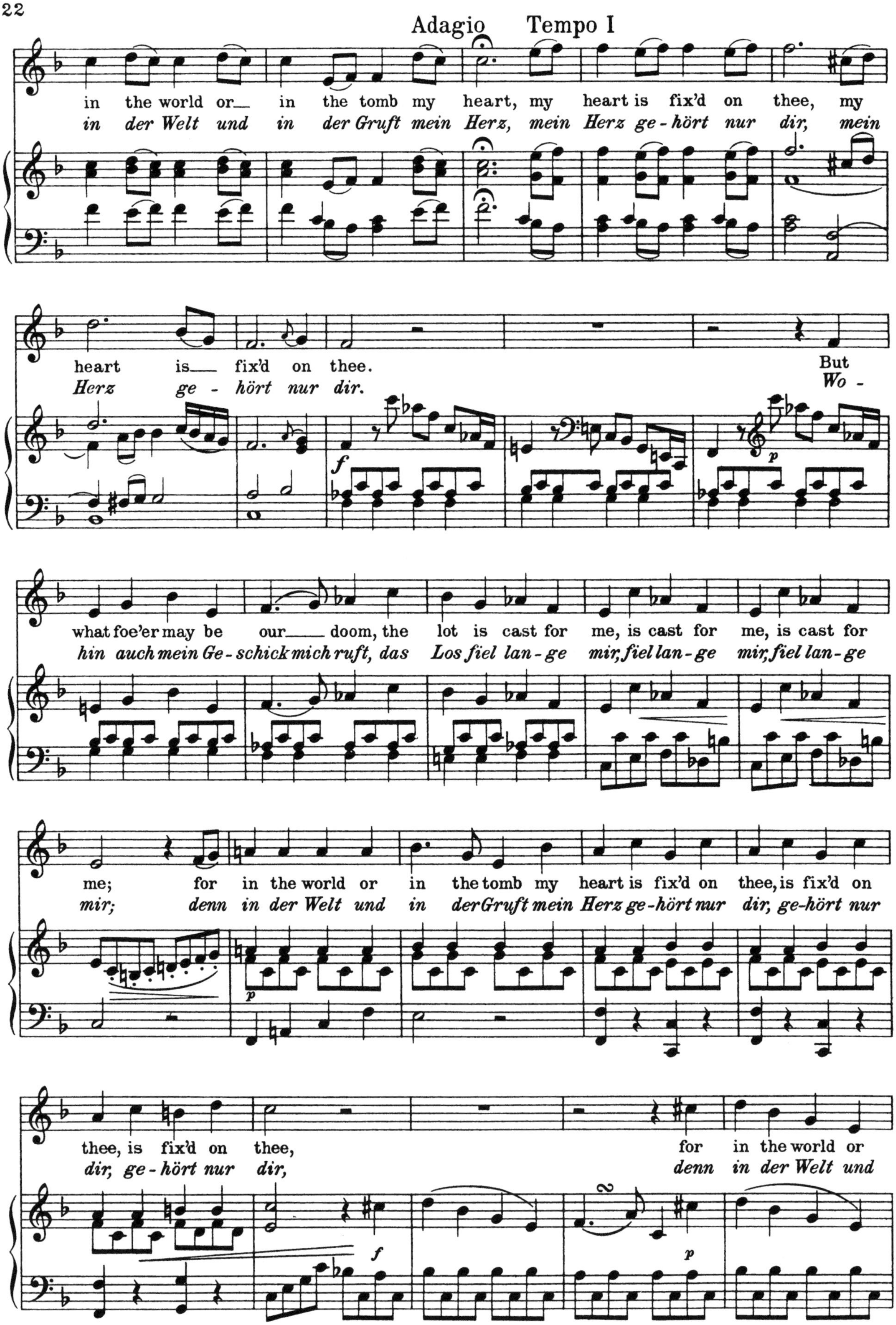
Adagio Tempo I
in the world or— in the tomb my heart, my heart is fix'd on thee, my
in der Welt und in der Gruft mein Herz, mein Herz ge - hört nur dir, mein
heart is— fix'd on thee. But
Herz ge - hört nur dir. Wo -
what foe'er may be our— doom, the lot is cast for me, is cast for me, is cast for
hin auch mein Ge - schick mich ruft, das Los fiel lan - ge mir, fiel lan - ge mir, fiel lan - ge
me; for in the world or in the tomb my heart is fix'd on thee, is fix'd on
mir; denn in der Welt und in der Gruft mein Herz ge - hört nur dir, ge - hört nur
thee, is fix'd on thee, for in the world or
dir, ge - hört nur dir, denn in der Welt und

Sailors Song / Englisches Matrosenlied

Glo- - - - -ry we maintain. Rattling ropes and rolling seas! Hur-ly bur-ly, hur-ly burly! War nor death can him displease, can him displease. Hur-ly bur-ly! Hur-ly bur-ly, hur-ly burly, hur-ly burly! War nor death can him displease, can him displease, can him dis-please.

Glo- - - - -rie un-be-siegt! Rassel Tau und rol-le Flut! Hur-re bur-re, hur-re burre! Krieg und Tod gefällt ihm gut, ge-fällt ihm gut. Hur-re bur-re! Hur-re burre, hurre burre, hurre burre! Krieg und Tod ge-fällt ihm gut, gefällt ihm gut, ge-fällt ihm gut.

The Wanderer / Der Wanderer

Sympathy / Sympathie

Translated from the Italian of Metastasio
Nach dem Italienischen des Metastasio

She never told her love / Die Liebe trug sie stumm

Piercing Eyes / Heller Blick

Content / Genügsamkeit

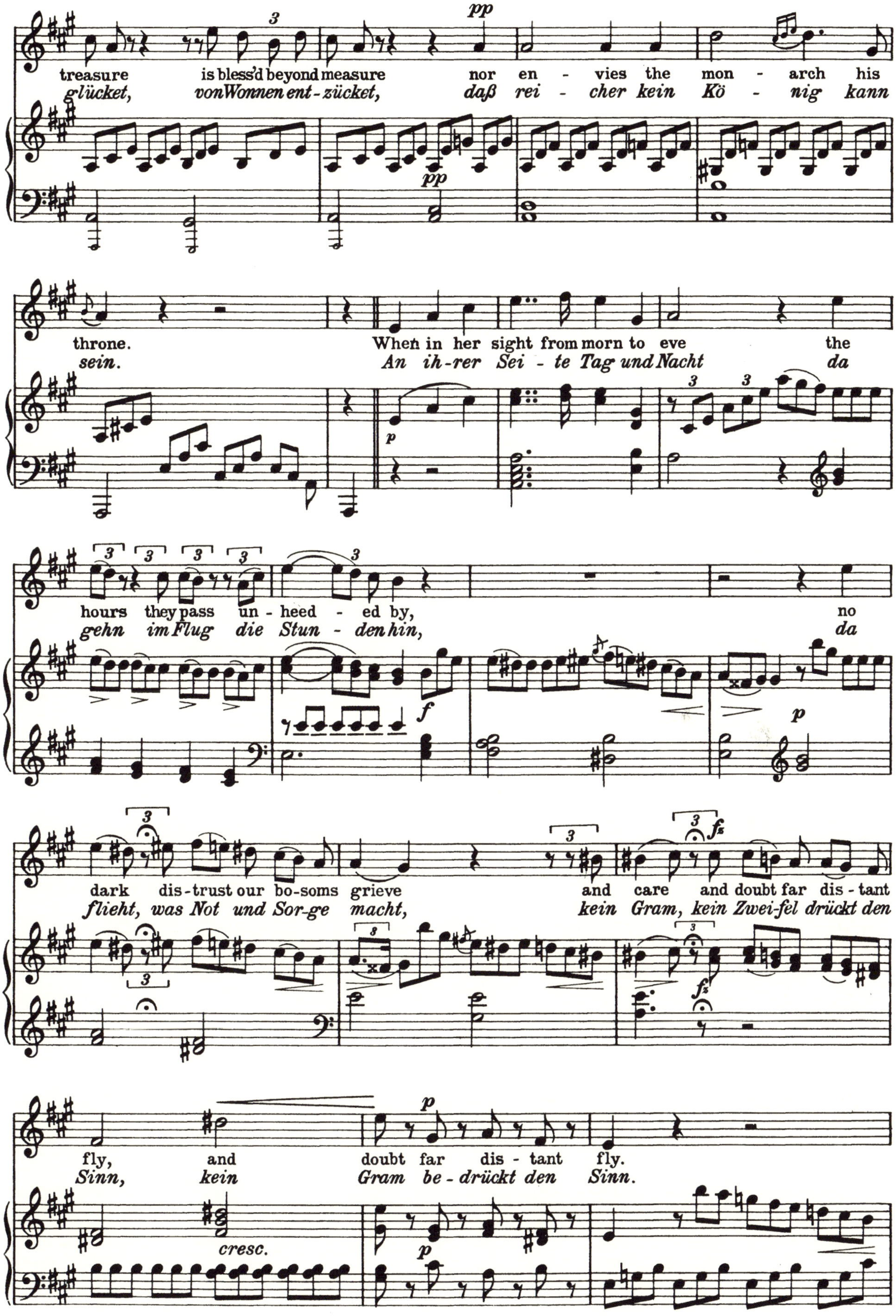
pp
treasure is bless'd beyond measure nor en - vies the mon - arch his
glücket, von Wonnen ent-zücket, daß rei - cher kein Kö - nig kann
pp
throne. When in her sight from morn to eve the
sein. An ih-rer Sei - te Tag und Nacht da
p
hours they pass un - heed - ed by, no
gehn im Flug die Stun - den hin, da
f
p
dark dis-trust our bo-soms grieve and care and doubt far dis - tant
flieht, was Not und Sor-ge macht, kein Gram, kein Zwei-fel drückt den
fz
fz
p
fly, and doubt far dis - tant fly.
Sinn, kein Gram be - drückt den Sinn.
cresc.
p

The Spirit's Song / Des Geistes Gesang

O tuneful Voice / O Stimme hold

Anne Hunter

Eine sehr gewöhnliche Geschichte

Christian Felix Weiße

3. Bekümmert will er wieder gehn,
   Da hört er schnell den Schlüssel drehn.
   |: Er hört: „Auf einen Augenblick,
   Doch geh auch gleich zurück!":|

4. Die Nachbarn plagt die Neugier sehr;
   Sie warteten der Wiederkehr.
   |: Er kam auch, doch erst morgens früh.
   Ei, ei, wie lachten sie! :|

Die Verlassene

Der Gleichsinn

J. J. Eschenburg

3. Reizend, zärtlich, fromm und reich,
Alles, Mädchen, gilt mir gleich.
Liebst du mich, so sterb ich eh,
Als ich dich verlassen seh.
Doch verachtest du mein Flehn,
Wohl, auch ich kann dich verschmähn!
|: Wenn dein Herz für mich nicht ist,
Was frag ich, für wen du bist! :|

An Thyrsis

Marianne von Ziegler

3. Ach, an meinem jungen Leben
   Zehret schon der Liebe Gram.
   Sagt, er soll mir wiedergeben,
   Was er mir so grausam nahm;
   Soll mich länger nicht mehr kränken;
   Denn ich könnt im Bach der Flur
   Mich und meinen Gram versenken —
   Doch im Traume könnt ich's nur.

Trost unglücklicher Liebe

Die Landlust

Stahl

3. So fern von Harm und Neide
   Scherz ich bei Lieb und Freude
   Mit unbewölktem Sinn
   Froh meine Tage hin.
   |: Mir blühet nie vergebens :|
   Ein Blümchen auf der Flur;
   Ich nütz die Zeit des Lebens;
   |: Denn einmal lebt man nur. :|

Die zu späte Ankunft der Mutter

3. Von Lenz und von Liebe gerühret,
Ward Hylas zum Küssen verführet.
|: Er küßte sie, er drückte sie,
Daß sie um Hülfe schrie. :|

4. Die Mutter kam eilend und fragte,
Was Hylas für Frevel hier wagte?
|: Die Tochter rief: „Es ist geschehn;
Ihr könnt nun wieder gehn. :|

Jeder meint, der Gegenstand_

Lachet nicht, Mädchen!

3. :|: Seh ich den Schäfer,
   Schön wie der Morgen,
   Irret mich das? :|
   :|: Sag ich nicht immer:
   Wohl mir! ich liebe,
   Liebe dich nicht? :|

4. :|: So oft ich sage:
   Wohl mir! ich liebe,
   Schäfer, dich nicht, :|
   :|: Schwellen den Busen,
   Heimliche Seufzer:
   Fürcht ich umsonst? :|

3. Dann, o Himmel, außer sich
   Würde ganz mein Herz zerlodern!
   |: Lieb und Leben könnt ich dich
   Nicht vergebens lassen fodern! :|

4. Gegengunst erhöhet Gunst,
   Liebe nähret Gegenliebe
   |: Und entflammt zu Feuersbrunst,
   Was ein Aschenfünkchen bliebe. :|

Gebet zu Gott

Auch die Sprödeste der Schönen

F. W. Gotter

3. Nichts verschont auf seinen Wegen
   Der Gewitterstrom im Hain;
   Tröpfelnd dringt ein Frühlingsregen
   Nach und nach in Felsen ein.

Zufriedenheit

Gleim

3. Und nach der Arbeit Ruh ist doch
   Der Arbeit bester Lohn.
   Ich mag es nicht, das Sklavenjoch,
   Geknüpft an eine Kron!

4. Als König hat er nichts als Schein;
   Und hat er was als Held?
   Ich wollte ja nicht König sein
   Um alles auf der Welt.

Das Leben ist ein Traum

Gleim

Lob der Faulheit

Lessing

Auf meines Vaters Grab

3. Ruhet wohl in euren stillen Grüften,
Die ihr edel wart und fromm wie er!
Gottes Friede weh in Blumendüften
Über eure Ruhestellen her!

Un tetto umil / Ein kleines Haus

Antwort auf die Frage eines Mädchens / Pensi a me sì fido amante

In nomine Domini

Abschiedslied

Gott, erhalte den Kaiser!

Lorenz Leopold Haschka

3. Ströme deiner Gaben Fülle
Über Ihn, Sein Haus und Reich!
Brich der Bosheit Macht, enthülle
Jeden Schelm= und Buben=Streich!
Dein Gesetz sei stets Sein Wille,
Dieser uns Gesetzen gleich!
Gott, erhalte Franz den Kaiser,
Unsern guten Kaiser Franz!

4. Froh erleb Er Seinem Lande,
Seiner Völker höchsten Flor!
Seh sie, Eins durch Bruder=Bande,
Ragen allen andern vor,
Und vernehme noch am Rande
Später Gruft der Enkel Chor!
Gott, erhalte Franz den Kaiser,
Unsern guten Kaiser Franz!

REMARKS

Nos. 1—6.

Adapted from: a) "Dr Haydn's six original Canzonettas, for Voice with an accompaniment for the Pianoforte, dedicated to Mrs John Hunter, ... Printed for the author and sold by him ..." ⟨1794⟩.

Plate-number is missing. The few preserved copies of this original impression bear Haydn's personal signature. A second edition taken from the same plates appeared as: "First set, 1796" only with the alteration of the publisher's name, i. e. "Printed for Corri, Duszek & Co."

b) "Six Songs for Voice with Pianoforte accompaniment". Music by Joseph Haydn. Part III. Publishers, Artaria & Co., Vienna. August 1794. Plate No. 496. Quarto. The original English text is missing, on Haydn's personal authority these poems were translated into German in London.

c) "Oeuvres de J. Haydn. Cahier 9. Contenant 33 Airs et Chansons avec accompagnement du Pianoforte". Title overleaf ⟨in German⟩ 'Songs with Pianoforte' accompaniment by Joseph Haydn — Title in copper — Breitkopf & Haertel in Leipzig ⟨1803⟩. Printed in type. Quarto, under Nos. 18—23. This edition again only prints the German text, similar to b⟩.

During his first stay in London, a very warm friendship sprang up between Haydn, and the famous surgeon John Hunter and his wife Anne, a noted poetess.

Archdeacon Nares in an essay, signed N. in the Quarterly Musical Magazine and Review dealing with the English Canzonettas, pays this lady the compliment of being "a very ingenious poetess", he also discloses the information that Anne Hunter, to whom the music was dedicated, was the anonymous authoress of the poems, — that she had also used the poem of the 3rd Canzonetta, — A Pastoral Song — as a text for an Andante melody taken frome one of Pleyel's Sonatas and that Haydn with her consent had reversed the original order of the two verses.

Nos. 7—12.

Adapted from: a) "The Second Set of Dr Haydn's Original Canzonettas, for the Voice with a Pianoforte accompaniment, dedicated to the Right Hon. Lady Charlotte Bertie. ... Printed and Sold for Messrs Corri, Duszek & Co., London." Plate No. 537.

b) ⟨in German⟩ Six Songs to be sung with Pianoforte accompaniment, English and German text. The music by Herr Joseph Haydn. Part 4. Artaria & Co., Vienna. July 1798. Plate No. 754. Quarto.

c) "Oeuvres de J. Haydn. Cahier 8. 15 Airs et Chansons et Arianne à Naxos, Scène avec accompagnement du Pianoforte." Title overleaf, ⟨in German⟩: Songs with Pianoforte accompaniment by Joseph Haydn. — Title in copper — Breitkopf & Haertel, Leipzig 1803. Printed in type. Quarto. The Songs Nos. 7—11 in our edition are given in the former version as Nos. 11—15, No. 12 in Volume 9 of the same edition is printed with Nos. 1—6. Both sets reprint the songs without the original English text, but substitute a new translation in its place. The song "Sympathy" had been published as a supplement No. 12 ⟨with the same English version⟩ to the Allgemeine Musikalische Zeitung in 1799, Rochlitz in No. 28 of this periodical disclosed the information that it had been anonymously translated by a certain Dr. Jaeger. The verses of song No. 10 are taken from the 4th scene, Act 2, of Shakespeares's Comedy, "As you like it".

They formulate Viola's answer to the question of the Duke regarding the existence of her alleged sister.

No. 13.

Adapted from: "The Spirit's Song", German — "Des Geistes Gesang" ⟨in German⟩. Poem by Shakespeare, with German and English text, set to music by Joseph Haydn. Publishers — The Comptoir for Industry and Art, Vienna. 1804. Plate Nr. 303. Quarto. The date of its appearance is proved by a review in the Allgemeine Musikalische Zeitung, Volume 6, No. 12 of March 1804. The song was most probably written shortly after or during Haydn's second stay in London. Any definite verification of the title, that the verses are Shakespearean in origin, could not be substantiated It is most likely an error on Haydn's part, he was then 74 years of age and unable to trust his memory.

The ossianic mood and style of language exhibited rather reflect the work of an author of the last decade of the 18th century.

No. 14.

Adapted from: "O tuneful voice". German — "O süsser Ton" ⟨in German⟩. Song with Pianoforte accompaniment, set to music by Joseph Haydn, Leipzig. Breitkopf & Haertel. ... 1806. Printed in type.

At the same time as this song was written, Anne Hunter bade farewell to Haydn ⟨See remarks 1—6⟩, who left London finally in August 1795. This song was also set to music for his friend, although no publication of it was contemplated at the time. A whole ten years elapsed before he was requested by Clementi, who at the time was partner in a music publishing firm in London, to hand him over the manuscript. After having brought it to light again, he offered it first to his publishers Breitkopf & Haertel who produced it early in 1806. ⟨Reference: Review by Rochlitz in the Allgemeine Musikalische Zeitung, Volume 8, No. 23. March 1806⟩. An English edition of it appeared a little later published by Clementi, Banger, Hyde, Collard & Davis in London.

Nos. 15—30.

Adapted from: a) "Twelve Songs for Pianoforte, Most affectionately and respectfully dedicated to Francisca Liebe v. Kreutznern by Joseph Haydn, Conductor to the Court of Prince Esterhazy. Printed and Published by Artaria & Co., Vienna".

Nos. 15—21 of our selection have been drawn from the first half of the above publication which appeared in December 1781. The second half was published two years later and bore the same title. It contains Nos. 22—30 of the collection under discussion.

b) Complete edition of 1803. Volume 9. Title as before.

c) The complete edition reprinted only 20 of the original 24 belonging to the first two collections by Artaria, one of which — No. 22 in our edition, — was supplied with a new text. Amongst those omitted were Nos. 19 and 26 of the selection under discussion, entitled, "Solace for unrequited Love" — "Trost unglücklicher Liebe" and "The shyest Beauty" — "Die Sprödeste der Schönen". Both songs are for this reason missing in the old Peters Edition, the editor had evidently not known or made use of them.

Anton Liebe v. Kreutznern, head of the Commissariat for Army Canteens was the father of the lady to whom the songs were dedicated, he had at one time commissioned Haydn to write the well-known Mariazell Mass. Haydn had laid great stress on the importance of the songs belonging to the first collection. He was convinced, as he wrote to Artaria, "that by reason of their easy, varied and natural treatment, they would be more suitable to the voice than any he had ever written before". The somewhat risky Roccoco Song "The mother's belated return", No. 21, caused Haydn some concern, as he felt that it would not pass the rigorous censorship, — „It would seem a great pity" he continues in his letter to Artaria "as I have managed to write an air which suits the words extraordinarily well."

The censor, however turned out to be less of a prude than the subsequent publisher. The entire edition of 1803 cut the text with the exception of the first verse.

The second as well as the final verse evaded the risky section in the following manner:

They were locked in each other's arms,
While the Nightingale sang of their bliss,
Her Mother came, questioning: "What do you here?"
"Heed us not — he is protecting me".

This song was entirely suppressed by the old Peters edition, and for obviously similar reasons, the delightful song entitled "A Very Ordinary Affair" — German title: "Eine sehr gewöhnliche Geschichte" No. 15 — shared the same fate.

According to ⟨a⟩ the voice-part of No. 17: "Synonym" shows an interruption of two bars of piano interlude after every two verses. These interludes are missing, at ⟨a⟩ much to the advantage of its more easily flowing "bourgeois" tune.

Our edition for this reason has accepted this somewhat abridged version, a few verses have been omitted from the more lengthy and less important songs in order to avoid unnecessary heaviness. No. 30 has been deprived of three verses, Nos. 7 and 27 of two each and Nos. 19, 20, 23, 25 and 28, of one verse respectively.

No. 31.

Adapted from: Complete edition of 1803, Volume 8: for Title refer to ⟨c⟩ Nos. 7 to 12.

No. 32

Adapted from: Complete edition of 1803, Volume 9, for Title refer to ⟨c⟩ Nos. 1 to 6.

⟨b⟩ an authorised copy, authorised by Haydn's own signature, is to be seen in the Music Department of the Prussian State Library.

In the version ⟨a⟩ the Italian text is printed below the German text, version ⟨b⟩ gives the German text only. Notwithstanding it is not unlikely that the Italian verses form the original material and that the German text is adapted from them.

No. 33.

A copy made by C. F. Pohl from the autograph which in 1873 was in the possession of a certain Herr S. Tauber, a broker in Vienna. According to a note by Pohl this autograph bears Haydn's personal inscription:

"Joseph Haydn, 14. 10. 1790."

The circumstances surrounding this date which denotes the date prior to Haydn's first visit to London lend to the song the significance of a personal moral.

It is here published for the first time in print, the text of the second verse, here omitted, runs as follows:

"Avarice only spoils the pleasure
God hath given in such measure,
Robs us of the virtues all,
Makes us wretched, mean, and small."

No. 34.

Adapted from: The manuscript collection of one-part songs with pianoforte accompaniment, date, the end of the 18th and beginning of the 19th centuries, completely bound in fine leather with the initials E. H. V. B. inscribed in gold lettering on the front cover. Berlin. Music Department of the Prussian State Library. MS. 30159. Pages 202 and 203. Haydn's name is not given.

This collection does however, include two other songs by him: "To Iris", ⟨German⟩ "An Iris", printed for the first time by Artaria, and included in their first collection in 1782, author — anonymous, as well as the song "To Friendship" which had made its appearance for the first time in the old Peters' edition with Haydn's name as composer. This is given in slightly altered form on page 209. Following this we find a very popular old time aria entitled: "Life's Troubles", from the musical comedy: "The Little Sailor Man", a German adaptation by Herklots, of Gaveaux's Operetta "Le Petit Matelot" 1795. The inclusion of "The Song of Farewell" ten pages earlier must therefore have occurred fairly soon after its creation. This is the song which Haydn's biographer C. F. Pohl classifies as No. 26 on page 14 of the biography at the end of Volume 2 as "The Song of Farewell" for Frau von Genzinger, and which, on his authority, Haydn is supposed to have dedicated to this friend prior to his first journey to England. ⟨Pohl's Biography. Vol. 2 Page 234.⟩ Haydn carried on a considerable correspondence with her when in London and Esterhaz, this has been preserved and was first published by Karajan.

There exists only a single copy of this song which is practically unknown in Germany, it was published in April 1882 by Augener & Co., London, supplied with an English and German text and entitled "Song of Farewell, dedicated to his friend Marianne von Genzinger with pianoforte accompaniment by Joseph Haydn".

The remark on the last page — for particulars about this song see Haydn's biography by C. F. Pohl, Volume 2, page 234 — seems to suggest that Pohl had some personal connection with the printers, he may even have been the actual publisher.

Haydn's last will and testament contains a copy of this song, dated 12. 2. 85, written in his own hand and which, apart from a few added marks of expression and slurs, seems to coincide exactly with the printed edition.

Pohl heads the copy with the remark "In the possession of Anton Ruthner, who received it from the Vicar of

Seefeld, who in turn acquired it from Frau von Genzinger". Remark No. 7, on page 234 of this Biography informs us that Pohl did not come into first-hand possession of the song but by way of Herr F. Wessely, music dealer in Vienna.

It goes on to relate that "The owner of the song, a man already well on in years, had journeyed from the country into the town in order to draw people's attention to it, ever since then however he had mysteriously disappeared". The whole matter becomes involved, as Pohl's copy, and Augener's engraving seem to tally tolerably well with the Berlin manuscript version, which was full of mistakes and evidently the work of an amateur.

All these modifications in text seem to suggest that alterations were made later.

It almost seems that some person undertook these "improvements" and wrote them in eighteenth century style, especially as certain passages were evidently considered too simple and wanting in finesse.

Here, for instance, are the first bars of the print in question:—

The effect of the two-part horn passage, in itself a delightful idea for a song of farewell is surely eliminated by the addition of a pedal bass, this persists on an octave F for three bars and finishes itself off in a rather clumsy fashion.

Added to this, the little half-bar interludes, so characteristic of Haydn, have been completely obliterated in the first phrase for the voice, the same applies to the tune which is so reminiscent of the Tamino Air ("The Magic Flute") in bars 14 and 15, and which must be attributed to his pen.

Such kindred ideas to those in some of Mozart's Operas, for which Haydn showed tremendous admiration and study, often occurred in the works written in his later years. Taking everything into consideration, I am of the opinion that the Berlin manuscript reproduces the most trustworthy version, it undoubtedly seems to be more closely related to the original than to the print of 1882.

Should the song however be one of Haydn's original compositions, and we have little reason to doubt this, (the Berlin manuscript and other characteristics rather points to this fact), and should the above passage, which bears such striking resemblance to bars 52 and 53 of the Tamino Air be only a musical coincidence, then Pohl's suggestion regarding its creation before Haydn's departure for England must be refuted, as "The Magic Flute" opera was written in the summer of the following year. Marianne von Genzinger's death on Jan. 23rd, 1793 also precludes the possibility of the song having been written as a farewell greeting on the occasion of Haydn's second journey to England in 1794.

Haydn had been staying in London for some time, during which the first performance of "The Magic Flute" had taken place in September 1791.

The reappearance of the autograph can only supply a solution of these various problems, we would express the hope that its present owner, having perused these explanations, will come forward and divulge its present whereabouts.

No. 35.

Adapted from: a) the autograph in the National Library at Vienna.

b) first impression: "Gott erhalte den Kaiser" — "God protect our Emperor" — Poem by Lorenz Leopold Haschka, set to music by Joseph Haydn.

"First performed in public February 12th 1797." Evidence as to edition or place of publication is not given. It apparently contains one phrase printed from a woodcut and one page printed from type.

During his stay in London, Haydn had not missed the opportunity of observing the profound effect of the English National Anthem. On his return home his desire was to create something of a similar nature for his Fatherland, and through his influence Haschka was commissioned by the Ministry to write the verses, which Haydn set to music in 1797.

The Anthem was subsequently sung on the 12th of February, the Emperor's birthday, in the Royal National Theatre, at Vienna, and at the same introduced to all Theatres in the Austrian Monarchy.

"Deutschland, Deutschland über Alles", Hoffmann von Fallersleben's well-known text, which has come to be associated with the German National Anthem, originated in 1841.